Slingshots and Love Plums

SLINGSHOTS
and love plums

POEMS BY
Wendy Videlock

ABLE MUSE PRESS

Able Muse Press

www.ablemusepress.com

Printed in the United States of America

Library of Congress Control Number: 2015931123

ISBN 978-1-927409-52-7 (paperback)
ISBN 978-1-927409-53-4 (digital)

Cover image: "Gesture Pose" by Mary Ellen Andrews

Cover & book design by Alexander Pepple

Able Muse Press is an imprint of *Able Muse:* A Review of Poetry, Prose & Art—at www.ablemuse.com

Able Muse Press
467 Saratoga Avenue #602
San Jose, CA 95129

for Terri

Acknowledgments

The author wishes to acknowledge the continued support of Alex Pepple, and the editors of the following journals, in which the following poems first appeared, sometimes in earlier versions:

Able Muse: "Invocation," "The Vigilantes," "In the Wind," "What the Sculptor Said."

American Arts Quarterly: "Lacuna."

Colorado Life Magazine: "In Escalante Canyon."

Hampden Sydney Poetry Review: "Sprig of Thyme," "Soft-Bellied Forgetful Things," "Poem for Maria," "Dear Ms. McFee."

Hopkins Review: "A Riddle," "I've Said the Words," "What the World Needs."

Hudson Review: "Dear Friends."

Kin: "El Alma del Oeste," "Nest, Empty," "The Ax," "On Being Asked Where I Have Been."

Marginalia: "From the Hollows."

New Criterion: "How You Might Approach a Foal," "To the Woman in the Garden," "By the Old River," "Nor What We Mean."

Poetry: "A Lizard in Spanish Valley," "Proverbial," "Bane," "!"

Quadrant: "The Consumer," "Sometimes Spring," "Dear Clive," "I Know You, Sister."

Rattle: "Of You," "Merchant Culture," "The Night Relies."

Terrain: "Old Flames."

Virginia Quarterly Review: "A Toast," "I Say Archetype."

Western Weird (Manifest West Series): "No Tobacco," "Where the Squirrel Lay Dead."

Thanks to editor Sherman Alexie for selecting "How You Might Approach a Foal" for republication in *The Best American Poetry 2015.*

Foreword

WENDY VIDELOCK'S THIRD FULL-LENGTH collection is cause for celebration. In this book she continues what she began in *Nevertheless*—finding new ways to make the tradition of epigrammatic wit ring, sing and occasionally sting. The precision of her language and the riddling turns of her observations work to reorder the ordinary into the odd but true, much like the epigrams of J.V. Cunningham, Dorothy Parker, or even Herrick. While her grand master may be Emily Dickinson, the extraordinary compression of her poems also evokes the ghost of Samuel Menashe.

An epigram is not exactly a lyric. It requires overt ingenuity along with grace. It announces its artifice at the same time as it seeks out truth. Wendy reminds us just how powerful every syllable must be if a poet is to take on this kind of work. An early poem in this collection, first published in *Hudson Review,* both makes and enacts these points:

Dear Friends,

Here lie the dreams we put to rest.
And there, the things we meant to say.
Further on, those bits of faith.

Mindless things, they bore no pain
and easily went to their graves.
It's we who are not quite the same.

What words are these that eulogize while denying themselves, returning us to whoever we may be, unspoken, unspeakable, reminding us of our failures and vitality all at once? Ingenuity, grace, artifice, balance, truth, a whiff of satirical accusation: wit. More, hers is not a wit motivated by hatred, contempt, or disgust, but rather by gentler observations of error. She is not exactly metaphysical, but the poems do offer a formal internal equilibrium while retaining their intensity.

Videlock arrests because she arrests the complacent drift of sense. She is so good at it that what begins as a taste for her work can quickly turn into a craving—for deliciously cryptic spiritual riddles. Consider another of the signature poems from this book, "Proverbial," which rightly first appeared in *Poetry:*

> It's always darkest before the leopard's kiss.
> Where there's smoke there is emphasis.
> A bird in the hand is bound for the stove.
> The pen is no mightier than the soul.

Wendy has characterized herself as a "formalish" poet, and this poem exemplifies that tendency, both rhyme and meter told slant. But more—the accessible, practical gallows humor of the third line anchors the more extravagant comedy of the surroundings. How can one resist the questions that grow out of these unspoken metaphors? In what way is a leopard's kiss like the absent dawn? Do leopards kiss? Is fire a form of emphasis? Is the sword a soul? How can one not think here of Matthew 10:34, King James Version: "Think not that I am come to send peace on earth: I came not to send peace, but a sword." The order and discipline of the verses allow the proverbs and their associations to detonate in ways that are meaningful, yet mysterious.

How does she do this? Note that it is the second half of each proverb that is disrupted, displacing the dawn, fire, the bush, and the sword—but this mysterious place is exactly where the end-stopped rhymes hit. Yes, a technique, a powerful verse technique, in which a meaningfulness that is deeply pleasurable and hard to explain emerges into language: poetry, not prose.

Videlock achieves the spiritual wit of "Proverbial" again and again, in poems like "These Are the Things I Think I Know," "Person of Interest," and "I Say Archetype." Yet then, as a counterweight, come poems such as "To the Woman in the Garden," and "Dear Ms. McFee," where Videlock's satirical arrow finds its target with a convincing thud. In these moments, she reminds me of Wallace Stevens or Marianne Moore, with their ringing affirmations of experience. Videlock's woman in the garden "did not notice the roses,/ the stones, or even/ the toad," presumably a real toad in this imaginary garden, but could only speak, instead, and at length "of the horrible/ horrible/ horrible world." Videlock is on the side of the toads.

There are many other kinds of poems here, from the raunchy parody of "!" to the ecstatic natural vision of "In Escalante Canyon," from the mystical cunning of "Invocation" to the ordinary sexuality of "Nest, Empty," with its middle-aged lovers one moment "subdued," and the next "suddenly lewd," presumably because they can be just so. Throughout there is vitality in the language, coupled with thoughtful intent. Her language does not merely describe or even respond to the world, but is so energetic and well-crafted that she brings something new to it at the same time as she honors it. Videlock is a maker and a shaper, possessing the kind of wit that confuses the senses only to return us to them. As Marianne Moore put it, she works

> [to] demand on the one hand,
> the raw material of poetry in
> all its rawness and
> that which is on the other hand
> genuine.

What more could one ask? These are poems which offer delight and wonder, from syllable to parable, from slingshot to love plum.

—David J. Rothman, author of *Part of the Darkness*

Contents

Invocations

Confiscations

Altercations

Correlations

Indications

We are a people wedded to the word.

— Jack Mueller

Invocations

The Lebanese Woman Speaks

I speak cat.

If
you don't know that
if you're inclined

think persian wine

think mosque and shroud
and dune and hand
and feline as

the features of
the land of sand

or go with crow
or mourning dove
or prussian
blue
I speak those too.

Proverbial

It's always darkest before the leopard's kiss.

Where there's smoke there is emphasis.

A bird in the hand is bound for the stove.

The pen is no mightier than the soul.

Never underestimate the nib of corruption.

Better late than suffer the long introduction.

All work and no play is the way of the sloth.

If you can dream it, bring the child the moth.

He is not wise that parrots the wise.

All that glitters has been revised.

An idle mind is a sign of the times.

The less things change the more we doubt design.

How You Might Approach a Foal

like a lagoon,
like a canoe,
like you

are part earth
and part moon,
like
a bloom,
like déjà vu,
like you

had never been
to the outer brink
or the inner Louvre,
like straw,
like air,
like your mother
had just this morning
braided a dream

into your hair,
like you

have nothing to do,
like you

have never heard
a sermon or
a scathing word,
like a fool,
like a pearl,
like you

are new to the world.

If I should answer with a patch of aspen,

it is not because I am an aspen.
If I should speak of sleep,
or smoke,
or consecrated weather,
it is not for lack of flesh
and matter. You who are stone,
or cottage, or grove,
or given to the mother tongue
needn't name yourselves.
We know who you are.

In the Hand Mirror

In the hand mirror
of all things
being relative

to fall, and spring,
things dim,

sky
high, or medium,
lies that sneaky
space between
dying

and disappearing,
rhyming

and exalted meaning,

buying into

and believing.

Invocation

The scent, the chase, the wound, the rain—
here lies
the sandhill crane that I became—

I, Coyote, most at home on the road,
   am the ghost

of Hermes and of Crazy Horse,
of spotted fish and figure eights,
     of damselfly

and coral snake—

the shifting shape which slithers in
to break apart
your theories and your stoic heart

is never home
     is always home
is most at home where a gathering storm
   and a whale bone
   upturn

a wisp of smoke
     and a stepping stone.

The World is Old

The world is old,
and we are old

and how—

patience, sister,
we

are the elders now.

Old Flames

You have passion,
he'd said.
You lack warmth,
claimed another.
You need,
said the one with the beard.
I am a link,
I'd said.
I am trade,
to the other.
Don't be fooled,
to the one with the beard.
We are sex,
he'd said.
You are brains,
grieved another.
We are one,
vowed the one with the beard.
We are jackals,
I'd said.
I am eggs,
to the other.
We are none,
to the one with the beard.

The Undertow

— for Shawnee

There are those who keel in the undertow
and those who float in the blue,
those who consult the ancient ones
and those who covet the new,

those who chatter the day away
and those whose words are few—
those who live for clarity
and those who misconstrue,

those who play their aces in spades
and those who pocket the fool,
those who forever will dwell in your heart
and those who pass on through.

Says the Artist

With the cat

I generally
concur:

stalk,
sleep,
pounce,

purr.

In the beginning was the word and the word was aardvark.
— Kimberly Copeland

Dear Reader,

Chances are good that one or the other
of us is somewhat rude, under the gun,
out to lunch, slumped at the desk or on the hunt
for the mother of the mother tongue,

the steep curve, the spawn that soothes
a savage herd, a thin slice
of quietude, someone to blame, something
to praise, the blistered hand of gratitude,

the root that slumbers in the earth, the cure,
the balm, the recipe, the *fiat lux,*
the pause that dawns when stumbling on
a fallen bird, the certain lure

the sailors heard, or anything
resembling the first, or the last word.

Sprig of Thyme

tangelo
and floating llama
what is seem

and what is drama
son of god
and gaia's daughter

what is stone
and what is water
sprig of time

and fallen aster
what is myth
and what is matter

here upon
a child's laughter
mother moon

and tail of tyger
twisted rope
and maddest hatter

cosmic egg
and holy splatter
looming form

and spiraled clatter
gate of horn
and pitter-patter.

Confiscations

Dear Friends,

Here lie the dreams we put to rest.
And there, the things we meant to say.
Further on, those bits of faith.

Mindless things, they bore no pain
and easily went to their graves.
It's we who are not quite the same.

Said Artemis to Venus

I'm so ancient
I'm so pagan

I'm so twee
    the feminine

isn't an ism to me.

Where the squirrel lay dead,

a riot of crows
breaking bread.

A Riddle

My people are junkies, mothers, drunks,
witches, oracles, lawyers, monks.
I slip from the lip and lap from the sea.
I am the boat, and the ghost personality.
I am not what you think, nor what you've thought.
I am the whore who won't be bought.
Behold my guardians and my slaves—

try as you will, this won't be contained.
I lie in wait beneath your bed.
I'm hovering just above your head.
I will strike from within and vanish whole.
I will resurrect in your begging bowl.

I am the root, the bronze, the papier-mâché—
I will plant you, I will plant you, I will take you away.

Dear Writers, I'm compiling the first in what I hope is a series of publications I'm calling Artists among Artists. *The theme for issue 1 is "Faggot Dinosaur." I hope to hear from you! Thank you and best wishes.*

 — Ali, Editor, *Artists among Artists*

!

I think that I shall never fear
a brontosaurus that is queer,

iguanodon as fetisheer,
a mammoth bringing up the rear,
an astrodon with extra gear,

metrosexual squirrel and deer,
a breeder with a dance career,
a fruit with cauliflower ear,

a lesbianic Chanticleer,
a grinning limpish-wristed Lear,
the weird one or the mutineer,

but those who perfectly adhere,
stay clear, stay clear, stay clear, stay clear.

From the Hollows

There was no moon. The night was dumb,
as if it, too, distrusted some

paltry thought. For all I knew,
this night had sought out cracks of blue

and holes of gold within its gut,
throughout its coves, then lost its love

of compromise or what is missing,
like half-closed eyes, and sweetly kissing.

Of You

— i.m.

You've been the wolf, you've been the bear,
you were the grass when I was air,
the hush of the lake, eyes and lips,
a shyness at my fingertips,

a motion that knew when to slow,
the forest where I always go;

and now you are the windowsill
I rest my elbows on until
the night grows dark and I can't see
these silhouettes of you and me.

I Know You, Sister

I know you, sister.
You're the one
who runs and runs.

And you as well,
mountain woman,
you speak the tongue;

your daughter is
the weightless one.
White witch,

bright queen,
I too have held
a box of stones

and called it gold.
Blue dreamer,
wife of mist,

I've slept your sleep,
I've kissed your kiss.
Man of silence,

man in the moon,
father winter,
warring fool,

alas, alas,
I know you, too.

No Tobacco

No tobacco,
No meat
No weed
no soda—

everybody
goin' yoga.

Do Not Return

Do not return, do not return
to the scene of the rebellion,
to the place of the defection,
to the one who meant to end you—
there will be no sign
of the you you left behind,
just a mountain to the west
and a sinking in your chest.

What the Sculptor Said

Given a whit of vision and precision,
a man can chip away at a thing,
revealing the shape that lies within:

Pallas Athena,

The Thinker, The Kiss,

The Griffin's Wing.

Given this inexplicable itch
to know the shape that lies within
(by chipping and chipping away at a thing),

it's wise to recall

this can also result

in nothing at all.

The Consumer

The consumer will paint your face.
The consumer will slip and slide.
The consumer will leave no trace.
The consumer will take you alive.

The consumer will lie in wait.
The consumer will give you a ride.
The consumer will fill your plate.
The consumer will take you alive.

The consumer will slither in.
The consumer will gaze in your eyes.
The consumer will always win.
The consumer will eat you alive.

If You Should See

If you should see the man I knew,
you needn't say my name aloud,
nor ask him why the white duck flew,

or what the water flower knows.
Do not sing to break his mood.
Don't offer him the mountain rose.

The aster and the muted bird,
the dress that's slowly lifted off,
don't mention these. Say not a word

of innocence or blue canoes.
Say nothing of the kited moon.
These things are mine, not his to lose.

In the waiting room,

no words
and violets in bloom.

In the Wind

— for Vin

In the wind, by the lake,
a friend
turns around
to say,
just so you know,

the wind carries your words away.

Poem for Maria

Just after the awful affair
she placed an aster in her hair
and jumped from the Mojo Bridge
to the sound of her fading laughter,
the aster falling just after.

Soft-Bellied Forgetful Things

Soft-bellied forgetful things,
what have you done with your dark queens
in their animal sleeves,
their thrones assembled of stones and twigs,
their crowns the braided synthesis
of roiling seas and river leaves.
Where have gone your fisher kings,
your trails of tears, your witches of stink—
their songs the storms of rag and weed.
What have you done with the worst of your fears,

the glass that breaks at the base of the brain,
the shadow-valley nobody's seen,
the pack of wolves which circles itself,
unspeakably tethered, unreachably steeped
in wilderness by word and stream.

Curiosity

Curiosity,
afraid
of its own shadow,

wages a strange
sort of battle.

The Ax

The long-standing juniper bush
got the ax from us this year.
We left the stump
      and made of it
a lantern and a cairn.
The neighbors stop and stare,
though not in horror,
      or despair.

May all my murders
be handled with such care.

Lacuna

It isn't that it's dark.
It's not that it's big.
It's the indigo in it
that sticks like a bitch.
The sad fact is
it's smaller than a fist.
Lighter than a chore.
It has no core.
The thing just is.
It's bona fide.
This doesn't mean
your hands are tied.
Declare yourself
a private war.
Sing to it.
Learn to fall
in love with it.
Throw open every door.
It might stick less.
It might stick
more.

Altercations

The Art Teacher

When Mr. Brooder bared his teeth

and growled at me (for I believed
what I perceived and fathomed red
in a patch of blue), I knew

the secret of him, and the secret of you.

Dear Clive,

We gentle readers dearly love
to tell you what we're made up of:
kindness, hugs, a slice of sun,

the best intentions (every one),
experience, serenity,
the wisdom that we all are one;

because of this we can't help note
that in the course of stanza four,
your narrator has squashed a bug—

it's sad to see you're not like us,
you heartless pig, you fucking slug.

The Purple Cantaloupe

Down at the Purple Cantaloupe,
the poet delivers an anecdote
as though it were his own.
He takes his glory à la mode,

and speaks to the peasants of mother lodes.
The moon looks to the calf and lows.
Just up the hill and down the road
a marionette has taken the load

from the shoulders of a binary code.
Umbrellas take to the streets in rows.
A little further up the slope,
the rain has stilled. A cherry grove

has hung its neck from the end of a rope,
producing a song of blood-red hope,
which stains the lips and shatters the bones,
no anecdote, no à la mode.

Kitsch

Kitsch is the absolute denial of shit.
— Milan Kundera

Pondering kitsch
and shit
as opposites
has left me none
the wiser:

one is plum
and one the fertilizer.

The Death of the Forest

Throughout these valleys, through these hills,
are leaves assuming fetal curls.
They crack and fall from the limb.
The wolf and moth are gone.
Only a few tree nymphs remain.
Slowed, they comb the forest floor,
collecting water-colored stones,
arranging rings and feeble shrines
in remembrance of all they've seen.
They grow thin in the thinning air
and sleep, clutching bouquets of reeds.

One, a small and arduous spirit,
watches a distant peak.
Perceiving a face in the shape of a stone,
she leans toward the eyes and waits.
She's dragged her hair in the milk of weeds,
has stroked her wrists with river-soaked leaves,
has drunk from the long tongue of the sun.
The others vanish, one by one,
gifting their bones to the ghostly oak.
She leans toward the eyes of a stone.

Without Warning

Without warning,
rocking chairs
that tell a story,

blades of grass
and morning glory,
corridors

and rivers forming,
arrowheads
and autumn storming,

broken hymn,
memento mori.

This elaborate world,

a plethora of miracles
and turds.

Everybody's a Critic

Sunny,
yes,
and a little too windy,

edgy,
sure,

and awfully trendy,

rhymed, yes—
like a machete,

eager, yes,
and a little too friendly,

earthy, yep,
with airs aplenty,
lengthy, yes,

and awfully empty.

The girl with Navajo hair,

leaning back in a chair
barely there.

If the Person That You Are

If the person that you are
with your victories
and scars
with your fears
and guiding stars
gazes out unto the world

from within the little furls
of a curtain
or a banner
and little do

you have to do
with sand, or wind,
or water,

the climate is not apt
to shift
nor your perspective alter.

December Missive

Good cheer,
gentle luck,

and may your holidays
not suck.

Henry and Annie

They reconcile their distances.
They settle for acres of meringue,
the licorice and mild spice
that grow like vines—
the maps that tell the world:
sporadic living space ahead.
Henry and Annie broke an oath.
Now, they're nothing but apologized.
Henry won't look inside her eyes,
and Annie never cries.
Collecting golden lorikeets
and little silver globes, he wraps
the vine around his ties, she strings
her shoes with licorice—
sweet nothings and meringue.
But Henry and Annie aren't so strange.
At dusk we all recall the dawn
and have no words for what's behind.
We wrap our darlings closer in
and spin our tales around the room,
carefully revised. Further out,
within the wind, a stranger truth
resides, like Cherokee,
remembering, and solitary skies.

The Vigilantes

— for Samuel

The vigilantes. They're the ones
who sneak up from behind and say
it takes a year of warm and cold
to string a house with twinkle lights,
to know the tiger from the corn,
to see the face within the stone
or taking shape within the clouds
is probably your own. The place
the vigilantes vanish in
is paper thin, and flecked with gold.
They sleep inside the triangle
which opens just before it folds.
Or falls, like snow. It's they who turn
the leaves to burnished bits of light.
They speak of wheat, but secretly.
The vigilantes stir the roots
of thunder trees, and underneath,
an ocean springs. Their storms will form
a shore where words escape their lips
to brutalize us with tenderness—
their pale gray afternoon eyes
trailing away like mayflies.

Nest, Empty

Let us read the papers, my dear,
let us discuss the news,
let us be subdued
and suddenly lewd.

To the Gardener in Early Spring

If all the snow set out to fall
around your home,
and slender rows of yellow globes
and lemon grass,
those delicate and tender-rooted
promises,
groveled low in their white deaths,
would you hold
your small boy's hand, or wring your own—
curse the snow
that spring allowed, then hope for roses,
rows of roses
in your bones, on your brow,
would you grieve,
would you grumble, would you snipe
I should have known.

To the Newly Enlightened One

But I do understand
and I don't disagree
that you're taking yourself
very seriously.

On the Back of a Mule

Sometimes, all these rhymes,

rhapsodized

or otherwise,
bodied forth
or of the soul,
flagrant or

metaphored,

in the trench

or far removed,
on the back of a mule

are sent to the moon,

who's often moved

to disapprove.

Correlations

In the shadow

of the old wheelbarrow
many leaves have fallen.

Person of Interest

I'm not the one who planted those snapdragons
and carefully placed those golden oaks in the yards
of unsuspecting strangers and I am not the one who
returned the spotted fawn to the fold, or slaughtered
the lust for power in the soul, nor am I the one
who brought back the bee and stopped the train
and painted the tracks blue I am innocent innocent I tell you.

Says the Lake

There are those

who

are shallow round
the edges,

others through and through.

In the country of appraising,

it seems we have exchanged
awesome for *amazing.*

The Busker from Conundrum

The busker from Conundrum has pruned
his rhododendrons and the woman
of the jewel

has become an ivory schooner
and the keepers at the gate
have replaced

their hands at poker while the swallows
take their baths in the black
bear's tracks

and the snooze button Buddhist has
drunk another nectar
and the working class

hero is receiving all his medals
and the crazy old witch
has scooped up all

the gardens and sent them to the lever,
singing, *don't you see*
don't you see

these ordinary little seeds
and scribbled little runes—

they were not used
for divination,
but for magic, fools.

In Escalante Canyon

In Escalante Canyon,
in between
the ten thousand
cottonwoods,

a muddy stream,
one young
big

horn,
many spotted calves,
a crumbled wall
of beer cans,
an overturned raft,

the desert and the snow,
the rapids and
the slow,
the ruined and
the wind
blown.

To the Woman in the Garden

You did not notice the roses,
the stones, or even
the toad, the child,
the sapling, the totem
pole, the crow, the dusk,
or the hummingbird,
the mantis, the dove,
or the hushed
word

but spoke instead,
but spoke at length
of the horrible
horrible
horrible world.

Sometimes Spring

I'm sometimes spring
and sometimes wintress,
sometimes bawdy,

sometimes impish,
sometimes skinny,
sometimes blimpish,

sometimes bored
and sometimes ravaged,
sometimes color,

sometimes language,
sometimes zen,
sometimes famished.

Bane

Full of strength and laced
with fragility:

the thoroughbred,
the hummingbird,
and all things
cursed
with agility.

What the World Needs

What the world needs
are bumblebees
and the strange vibe,

the slow saunter
and the ride,
fewer speeches,

more asides,
languid rhythms,
reckless tides,

revelation,
subtle find,

the stupid journey
and the wise,

a broken bridge
and a Blue Sage Drive.

A Toast

Here's to the innards
and übers
and blossoms
and tubers and under

whelmers and bent
fenders, the thin
senders and big
bangers,

the inner saints
and outer
rogues,
the great droughts
and great rains
and herons
and drakes
and outer crusts
and heavenly flakes

and inner little
earth
quakes.

Bum Foot

With my bum foot and busted pack
I make my way through the rains,
up a mountain,
into a cave,
out through a jungle,
into a haze.
I drag behind me
a bag of nails,
a feather,
a flute,
an anvil and
the mother root.

One is keenly aware
of distance with a bum foot.

On Glancing through My Son's World History Book

The most commonly
used words:

Rise,

Fall,

Merge.

The Night Relies

Beware the ones who fear the night.
We ghosts, Athena, Allah, Christ,

will take our place in the dark and fuse
the fodder, the mother, the mountain, the muse.
In sleep, we have no face to lose.

What's left is vague and sways the morning:
The camouflage is in conforming.

By noon we choose another word,
another myth, a lighter bird.
Between the train and bustling station

the human side of this equation:
when bathed by day or when in dream,
you are not you, nor who you seem;

the sum of what you think you've heard
will galvanize and will insist

a life will change inside the turn,
the night relies on what you've kissed—
the swollen moon, the creation myth,

the rain, the dusk, this rising mist.

I Say Archetype

I say archetype,
but I really mean messenger.

I say poet, but
I really mean bootlegger.

I say TSE, but secretly
I think I mean

The Mariner. I say fate,
mountain, river, wind,

when perhaps I mean inheritor.

Merchant Culture

What's the going rate for a poem these days?
　— JM

I'll trade you a drop of snow
for a lyrical poem,
a parking lot
for a river stone,
a soldier's heart
for a kettle of gold,
the justice card
for the nine of swords,
a Persian word
for an off-chord;
a thousand tears,
a thousand tomes
and a drop of snow
for a lyrical poem.

Broken Law

I do not seek them out, the stray cats,
the scattered and brawled, the unappalled,
the addicts and owls and moon kin—
they pitch on the rim at hard hours,
they loosen the screws and sun showers,
they live on the lamb, they drop in the lap—

perhaps
we love one another because
of our flaws,
says the outlaw to her dying pa—
would you like, says the ma,
some coleslaw. . . .

O ma—
I saw feral dogs and broken law
in Monument Valley and past the gulch,
throughout the gully, after the pause,
a hole in my craw, a burn in my belly
and all across the Hopi land,
Hopi music. Hopi sand.

The Temple on the Avenue

The temple on the avenue
where brown stones and dust accrue
is given to
the phantoms and their quiet rooms.

Indications

In a pale August glow,

a neighbor in his garden
weeding for Godot.

These Are the Things I Think I Know:

There's nothing whiter than the snow.
If it isn't a bridge, it's a puppet show.
There are single cells which intertwine.
There are yogis who have lost their minds.
You are not alone. You are not a twin.
Not every horse has the medicine.
There are towers that have no sense of time.
There are poets who cannot scan a line.
The end will place its bets on the start:
Beware the ram without an art.
The visions that will not meet the eye
will loom to remind you that you're blind.
The breeze that changes everything

will never stop to leave her name.
There are words that do not coincide.
There are students who cannot cross the divide.
The albatross that you will bear
will rob from the soul and give to the air.
Each poverty and heartache knows
the size of the kernel left in the bowl,
what to smash, and what to hone,
the ivory rib, and the goldilocks zone.

Exposed

Snow-wet, the maple is baring her old silhouette.
Soon this long-in-the-tooth philosopher moon
is certain to illuminate some other bloom.
Deep in the chest a creature sleeps, oblivious
to winter's net, in stark relief or silhouette.
Deeper still, another moon rolls a rune
into the night, no clattering, no sordid boon.

Nor What We Mean

We know no thing, nor what we mean.
Physician, tell the story of
the stoic ghost in the machine.

Remind us why and how all joys
and sorrows will rely on love.
Compare a harmony to noise,

reveal the seat of memory,
the streams and seas of consciousness,
the dream that dreamed assembly.

Explain the need for symbol, art,
for song, for dance. For violence.
Describe again the chambered heart.

Dear Ms. McFee,

When gathering up all your strength
for bringing airs and candied pears
to the sisters and elders on Wayfare,
you needn't brace, you needn't cringe
when someone has

an empathetic relapse,
when someone without malice laughs,
when someone tries to warm your hands.

You needn't sting the woman with
the decent man, nor snarl at
the elder with the face of sand,
nor curse a world that has no clue
what's right for them and right for you.

You needn't, but of course you can.

By the Old River

By the old river
in the middle
of winter
who is to say
who's modest
and who is opulent,
who is flute
and who is consonant,
who is greed
and who is salient,
who is rife
and who is somnolent,
who is clash
and who is complement.

The Poem As:

hurdy,
gurdy,
infomercial,
heart

of pearl and snapping
turtle,
florist,

tourist,
wild
mustard,
mortar, porter,
ghost

buster, wizard,
laser, fuck

of cluster,
peasant,
crescent,
feather

duster.

A Lizard in Spanish Valley

A lizard does not make a sound,
it has no song,
it does not share my love affairs
with flannel sheets,
bearded men, interlocking
silver rings, the moon,
the sea, or ink.

But sitting here this afternoon,
I've come to believe
we do share a love affair
and a belief—
in wink, blink, stone,
and heat.
Also, air.

This is not a fable,
nor is it bliss.

Impatience,
remember this.

The Pen Addresses the Poet

Lonely soul, where would you be
Without the humble likes of me—

No hopes of immortality,
No record of your gallantry,

No proof that you've crawled from the sea
And suffered so theatrically:

At my expense you guarantee
No thing but your own vanity—

Resist! Desist! Can you not see
Your vice will mean the end of me.

Spring Begins

Spring begins
and who could deny

hocus pocus,

pink sky,
ice floe,
wild crocus,

history blushing
like a bride,
a small stone
sewn into her side.

Averting the Gaze

Over the mountain, under siege,
a city emerges from the haze
to become the word of the hour,
an electronic tower, a blur,
a circuit, a gesture, something
akin to a flower.

The Mend

The clock is reeling through the air,
a leak is leaping from the pail,
the moon has rolled away the stair,

the poppies are rocking the rocking chair,
the crickets are courting the spectacled bear,
the aspen have eaten the magical pear,

leaving a hole in the pocket where
the fisherman's wife had patched a tear.

On Being Asked Where I Have Been

In a field of wheat,
on a dragon's tongue,
at the bottom of
a bottle of rum,
at the axiom
of a metaphor
and a bad pun,
at the loosening
of a baby tooth,
under a spell,
over the moon,
out of the blue,
at the quivering tip
of an arrow and
a bottom lip,
left behind,
at the canyon's whim,
on the back of the wind,
let loose,
taken in.

A Relevance

One
teeny tiny
worm

making the earth
turn.

I've Said the Words

I've said the words
but cannot know
what I've released

and what I keep,
what is chaff
and what is wheat,

or what of me
is satisfied
by errant vice

and put to sleep.

As November stirs,

the old pet learns
fewer and fewer words.

El Alma del Oeste

In recent weeks on shifting cliffs
at Canyonlands, or Rabbit Hill,
at Window Rock, or Wrinkled Sands,
or mesas where, this time of year,
slowly spill the waters,

we have sighted the claw of the infant spring
and heard the bighorn's hoof ring.
Like children we have peered into
the bed of the west, the canyon's rib,

and the empty nest. Like children we
have wondered who induced all this,
and what comes next.
And here we are, the two of us.
The lynx's prints at Corral Fork
have brought us to a cloud of quail.

We build a cairn and turn back to the trail.
A breeze can trade a mother's song
of letting go. *So shall ye sow.*
We speak in English, wind, and español.

WENDY VIDELOCK lives on the Western Slope of the Colorado Rockies. Her first full-length collection, *Nevertheless,* came out in 2011 and was a finalist for the 2012 Colorado Book Award, followed by *The Dark Gnu* in 2013, a book she illustrated. Her chapbook, *What's That Supposed to Mean,* appeared in 2009. Her poems have been published widely in literary journals, most notably in *Poetry* and *The New York Times.*

Also from Able Muse Press

William Baer, *Times Square and Other Stories*

Melissa Balmain, *Walking in on People – Poems*

Ben Berman, *Strange Borderlands – Poems*

Michael Cantor, *Life in the Second Circle – Poems*

Catherine Chandler, *Lines of Flight – Poems*

William Conelly, *Uncontested Grounds – Poems*

Maryann Corbett,
  Credo for the Checkout Line in Winter – Poems

John Philip Drury, *Sea Level Rising – Poems*

D.R. Goodman, *Greed: A Confession – Poems*

Margaret Ann Griffiths,
  Grasshopper – The Poetry of M A Griffiths

Jan D. Hodge, *Taking Shape – carmina figurata*

Ellen Kaufman, *House Music – Poems*

Carol Light, *Heaven from Steam – Poems*

April Lindner, *This Bed Our Bodies Shaped – Poems*

Martin McGovern, *Bad Fame – Poems*

Jeredith Merrin, *Cup – Poems*

Richard Newman,
  All the Wasted Beauty of the World – Poems

Frank Osen, *Virtue, Big as Sin – Poems*

Alexander Pepple (Editor), *Able Muse Anthology*

Alexander Pepple (Editor),
  Able Muse – a review of poetry, prose & art
  (semiannual issues, Winter 2010 onward)

James Pollock, *Sailing to Babylon – Poems*

Aaron Poochigian, *The Cosmic Purr – Poems*

John Ridland,
  Sir Gawain and the Green Knight – Translation

Stephen Scaer, *Pumpkin Chucking – Poems*

Hollis Seamon, *Corporeality – Stories*

Carrie Shipers, *Embarking on Catastrophe – Poems*

Matthew Buckley Smith,
  Dirge for an Imaginary World – Poems

Barbara Ellen Sorensen,
  Compositions of the Dead Playing Flutes – Poems

Wendy Videlock, *The Dark Gnu and Other Poems*

Wendy Videlock, *Nevertheless – Poems*

Richard Wakefield, *A Vertical Mile – Poems*

Gail White, *Asperity Street – Poems*

Chelsea Woodard, *Vellum – Poems*

www.ablemusepress.com

www.ingramcontent.com/pod-product-compliance
Lightning Source LLC
Chambersburg PA
CBHW021406090426
42742CB00009B/1033